NO TURNING Back

Jan
Van Hee

Sable Creek
PRESS
www.sablecreekpress.com

No Turning Back
The Life and Adventures of HERBERT ERNEST GRINGS
Missionary to the Belgian Congo, Africa

Based on the autobiography of Herbert E. Grings
December 16, 1892–November 7, 1977

Cover and text design by Diane King, www.dkingdesigner.com
Scripture taken from the King James Version. Public domain.
Published by Sable Creek Press, PO Box 12217, Glendale, Arizona 85318
www.sablecreekpress.com

Van Hee, Janis E.
    No turning back : the life and adventures of Herbert Grings missionary to the Congo / by Jan Van Hee.
    p. cm.
    ISBN 978-0-9766823-9-4
1. Grings, Herbert. 2. Missionaries—Congo (Democratic Republic)—Biography. 3. Missionaries—Africa—Biography. 4. Congo (Democratic Republic)—Description and travel. 5. Americans—Congo (Democratic Republic)—Biography. I. Title.
BV3625.C6 V36 2009
266/.0092—dc22   2009936863

Dedicated to

Winifred (Mrs. Bob) Grings who first introduced me to the story of her father-in-law and whose testimony was a great blessing to me,

and to

Louise (Grings) Champlin without whose valuable input and counsel this book would have been incomplete.

ACKNOWLEDGMENTS

Autobiography of Herbert Ernest Grings
Living Springs Printing Press
491-493 Chatham Road
Kowloon, Hong Kong

Missionary Heart Beats
by Louise Grings Champlin
IFM (Independent Fundamental Mission)
Greensboro, NC
(No date included)

TABLE OF CONTENTS

CHAPTER 1
TO LIVE OR DIE?

Herbert struggled to push the heavy wooden table from the side of the room and place it before the open window, where it would be visible to anyone passing by the house. Pain shot through him, and he felt like vomiting again. His strength ebbed from his body, though somehow he mustered enough energy to give the table one last shove.

"There! That should be close enough for passersby to see."

He crawled onto the table and lay down, with the tin can containing the dead poisonous adder nearby.

"I should have known better than to step down into the secret hold without checking first," he chided himself, "especially after having been away with it closed up for so long."

When he realized the adder had bitten him, Herbert was sure he would die. He knelt down and prayed, telling the Lord he was not afraid to die because he knew Jesus Christ had saved him. It appeared to him that Heaven opened to receive him and he was willing to go. However, a voice whispered to his heart, "But what will become of your children who expect you to meet them at the railroad station?"

"Yes, Lord, for my children's sake, heal me of this snakebite," he prayed, and he knew at once that he would not die.

The fever and pain tormented his mind and body throughout the long night. He prayed and sang as well as he could; all the while memories whirled in his mind. At first, his thoughts came at random...flames leapt toward him...the old man fiddled...Pygmies chased Herbert...he and Ruth stood before the government official who would marry them—his beloved Ruth!...waves smashed against the lifeboat...the children laughed and played in the shade of the trees that Ruth had planted...a huge python slithered toward him and raised its ugly head to strike...pincher ants swarmed everywhere.

Later the memories arose as the events had occurred. Herbert remembered his mother grieving over the death of his sister. He remembered her bending over the old metal, ribbed washboard, doing the laundry. He saw her wiping perspiration from her brow as she stood at the ironing board, pressing piles of clothes that belonged to an employer, trying to earn a living for the two of them after his father left.

Herbert Grings was ten years old again, the age when his life of joy and adventure began . . .

CHAPTER 2

DECISIONS

Ten-year-old Herbert Grings sat all week in the revival services in the big tent. He felt a struggle going on in his heart each night as the preacher invited people to come forward and give their hearts to the Lord Jesus who loved them and had given His life as payment for their sins. The last night of the meetings came and Herbert was afraid. He was afraid to give his heart to God because he didn't understand what God would require of him, though he was even more scared that God would shut the door of salvation, leaving him outside.

Herbert suddenly realized he had left his seat and was walking down the aisle with tears streaming down his cheeks. A kindly gentleman knelt beside him at the altar. The man explained that Herbert needed to confess to God that he was a sinner and to believe that God's Son, Jesus, had paid for his sins upon the cross and had then risen from the dead. The man said God would give Herbert the gift of eternal life if he would truly trust Christ Jesus to save him. That's exactly what Herbert chose to do. At once, his fears were gone and he knew a joy and happiness he had never known before.

The next day, Herbert told his schoolmates what he had done. They laughed and ridiculed him. "Ol' Herbie has gone and got religion," and "Are you gonna be a Sunday school sissy?" they taunted. Their reaction surprised Herbert. He knew he had trusted Jesus and was excited about living for Him. He only wanted to share his new joy with his classmates.

Undaunted in his new faith, however, Herbert was more determined than ever to live for the Lord. Even though he was a new Christian, he understood that pleasing God was more important than pleasing people. Since he did not yet attend church regularly, he consulted the pastor of a nearby church about the teasing.

The gray-headed, old minister said, "Well, Herbert, we have to suffer persecution if we serve the Lord Jesus." Herbert made another decision that day. He would take a stand for Jesus and share his faith, no matter what!

When he was much younger, Herbert's older sister died. Later, his parents divorced, and Herbert lived with his mother. They frequently moved from place to place, settling wherever his mother could find work. Divorce was very uncommon in that day and women had a difficult time earning a living. Herbert's mother worked cleaning, cooking, washing and ironing for other families, and though life was sometimes hard for him and his mother, Herbert did not dwell on the hardships.

Eventually his mother married a widowed farmer for whom she worked. The union was a happy one for all involved and Herbert now had two stepbrothers.

Wherever they lived, Herbert tried to be in church and to be involved in the youth group. He was a good student and aspired to get a higher education. He left the farm after high school graduation and attended business college where he took a stenographer's course. When he was eighteen years old, he joined the United States Navy. Each time his ship docked, Herbert sought Christian groups where he could fellowship with other believers. While in one port, a Christian lady gave him a nice, leather bound Bible. How Herbert treasured that

Bible, the first one he ever owned! He cherished it and, as a testimony of his faith in the God it told about, he boldly and openly read it on the ship.

Herbert did well in the Navy and planned to make a career in it. Near the end of his fourth year, he transferred to a torpedo boat destroyer where he served as a paymaster's assistant and was up for a promotion. The ship docked in San Diego harbor and one night while most of the crew had gone ashore, Herbert sat in his little office reading his Bible.

That night the Lord spoke to his heart saying, "Choose now whether you are going to be Paymaster's Clerk or follow me."

Herbert knelt beside his chair and dedicated his life to serving God. He turned his back on his Navy career and never regretted that decision.

Herbert was in love with a young woman and looked forward to marrying her. However, when she learned of his decision to serve God, she broke up with him and married another young man. Although he was deeply hurt, Herbert decided it was for the best. "I will never let the feminine charms of a woman keep me from serving God," he decided.

As soon as he received his honorable discharge from the Navy, Herbert headed straight for Bible school, arriving just before the fall term opened. He had saved a little over seven hundred dollars from his Navy salary, which was enough to pay all his expenses.

A whole new and wonderful life opened up to Herbert as he began his studies and became acquainted with many of the other students—all were dedicated to the Lord Jesus, desiring to know Him better and to make Him known to others. Herbert eagerly immersed himself in his studies. His spiritual life grew and his burden for lost souls increased. He found great joy in giving out tracts, testifying in street meetings and streetcar barns and preaching God's Word at every opportunity. He preached his first sermon in a mission hall. He joined a group called "The Fishermen's Club." Led by a man named Daddy Horton, the group met every week for supper and Bible study.

One night Daddy Horton preached on the text: "Woe is me if I preach not the Gospel." He stretched out his hands over the young men's heads and said, "Oh, that I could put some of that woe upon you, young men!"

Herbert later said, "Truly it fell upon me. I cannot look upon a crowd of people without wanting to preach to them."

One of the young men from the Fishermen's Club went as a missionary to the natives of British East Africa. While there, he became ill with a fever and died. The call came back to the others in the club, "Who is going to take his place?" Herbert knew that call was for him. He immediately volunteered and began to pray and plan to go to Africa. He applied to the Africa Inland Mission but did not receive a reply. After graduating from Bible College, he decided to take the first opportunity to preach the Gospel while he waited for the door to Africa to open.

One day while Herbert waited to hear from the mission board, Daddy Horton telephoned.

"Herbert," he said, "a group of churches want to send a man to start a Sunday school among the mountain people in the redwood forests of Mendocino County, California. I believe you are just the man we are looking for. Would you be willing to go?"

"Yes, Sir!" Herbert answered.

"How soon can you be ready to go?"

"I can be there in two weeks," Herbert replied.

The group gave him a horse and forty dollars a month. He packed an extra pair of socks and an extra shirt in one side of his saddlebag, his Bible and gospel literature in the other, and started up the mountain trail on his horse.

Herbert met some wild folks on those mountain trails. One man was a criminal from the East who fled to the redwood forest to escape the law. He allowed his wife to feed Herbert and give him a place to sleep, but said he did not want to hear the name of God in his house. One evening when Herbert was visiting in the log cabin where this family lived, a group of young people came to the house. The old man got out his fiddle and started to play. The young people began to dance. Herbert sat on a bench alone. Since there were an odd number of dancers, throughout the evening almost everyone took a turn sitting beside Herbert. He talked to each one who sat beside him about that person's need to trust Jesus, and the old man never heard a word!

For nearly a year, Herbert rode his horse over the mountain trails, holding meetings, organizing Sunday schools and witnessing in homes and on the trails. One day he received a letter from the group of churches that had sent him to the mountain people. They wrote that he would have to turn in his horse and quit, as they no longer had the money to support him.

Herbert said, "You can have my horse, but I'm not going to quit."

He returned his horse, threw his saddlebag over his shoulder and continued on foot, telling the mountain people about Jesus.

One day Herbert received a letter from Africa Inland Mission saying they had accepted him as a missionary to the Belgian Congo, and he should come to Los Angeles at once to make preparations. Herbert found he had mixed feelings. He dreaded saying goodbye to the mountain people, although he knew it was God's will for him to go to Africa. He decided to leave for Los Angeles immediately en route to New York, but he had no money for the trip. Then he opened another letter that had arrived in the same mail delivery. It contained a check for ten dollars—enough to get him to San Francisco—where he stopped to see his father, who worked there. His father was glad to know that Herbert was going to be a missionary. Herbert said nothing to him about needing money, yet his father gave him a ten-dollar gold-piece, which paid his way to Los Angeles.

At Los Angeles Herbert went to the Bible Institute and inquired if there was any mail for him, not really expecting any. After all, he had been away for a year. The clerk looked in the box and handed Herbert a letter that someone had sent weeks before hoping it would reach him at that address. The check that fell out of it was sufficient to pay his board and room until he could leave for the Africa Inland Mission headquarters in Brooklyn, New York.

CHAPTER 3
AFRICA AT LAST

A few weeks later, in June of 1917, forty-six young men and women, some of whom were married couples, gathered in Brooklyn, New York, to meet with the director of the Africa Inland Mission. The plan was to establish a chain of mission stations from Kasengu on the east border of the Congo to Lake Chad in French Equatorial Africa. Two separate groups were soon sent out, but Herbert and another young man, two young ladies and a married couple were held back. Herbert was keenly disappointed not to be among the first to leave; still he thanked God even though he did not understand why he could not go.

The world was at war—World War I—and it was dangerous to travel the seas. The first party of seventeen missionaries left for Africa on a British freighter and, just as they thought they had made it safely through all the mines and submarines scattered across the ocean and were in sight of Cape Town, Africa, the ship struck a mine. It sank within minutes. Lifeboats rescued the missionaries who endured much suffering in the cold waters before a tugboat picked them up. They lost all their baggage and gear. When Herbert heard this news, though he was grieved for the other missionaries, he thanked the Lord for holding him back.

The second party, made up of twenty-five missionaries and the General Director, Dr. Hurlburt, left on a British ship. They were at sea only a week when the coalbunkers caught fire and threatened to destroy the ship. The missionaries prayed and the crew brought the fire under control. The ship had to put in to a South American port for reconditioning. This delay in the trip cost the missionaries a great deal of extra expense and trials. Again, when Herbert heard the news, he was saddened for his fellow missionaries, though he thanked the Lord for sparing him the hardships.

"Were these the reasons God had not allowed him to go with one of the first groups?" he wondered.

It would be quite some time before Herbert learned the real reason God wanted him to wait and go with the last little party of four that included two young ladies, Margaret Moore and Ruth G. Fuller, another young man, Fay Tyler, and himself. They were chaperoned by a missionary couple, Mr. and Mrs. Hold.

While Herbert and the others awaited their turn to go to the Congo, they had an opportunity to become better acquainted. One of the young women, Ruth Fuller, sat by Herbert each evening at dinner. Ruth was a lovely Christian woman with light, golden-brown hair and sparkling green eyes. She was charming and well educated. More important than her loveliness was her caring, sensitive spirit and complete surrender to God. Herbert, however, had made up his mind that no woman's loveliness would distract him, so he hardly noticed either Ruth's outer or inner beauty. She learned that Herbert did not have a sun helmet in his outfit and secretly bought him one. Herbert thought one of the young men must have purchased it.

Ruth Fuller was born on December 5, 1888, in Garretsville, Ohio. She grew up in a Christian home with one brother and a sister. With her family, she actively attended church and tried to live according to God's Word. After high school, she attended Moody Bible Institute. She already felt God was calling her to be a missionary. After graduating, she went to Bozeman, Montana, where her parents had already moved to be missionaries to the Indians, and she taught in the school. Teaching prepared her well for the next step in her life, when she volunteered in 1917 to go to Africa as a missionary with the Africa Inland Mission. She knew that it would be a difficult life for a woman on such a primitive mission field; still Ruth loved the Lord and was determined to serve Him wherever He asked her to go. Thus, she and Herbert ended up going to Africa at the same time with the same mission board.

At last, the final group of missionaries left for the Congo on the British ship, City of Lahore. The voyage, which took twenty-one days, was uneventful. Even though Herbert enjoyed being back at sea, the voyage seemed unbearably long because he was eager to arrive at their destination. Finally, the trip was over and Herbert could set foot on African soil. Upon arrival, the group joined some of the missionaries who had arrived earlier. How excited Herbert and his companions were to hear of the earlier missionaries' experiences and plans. Herbert could hardly wait to start learning the language and preaching to the native people.

One of Herbert's first tasks as a missionary was to help with the funeral of a missionary wife who took ill with a fever and died. Soon two other missionaries died. Herbert quickly learned that death for the missionaries was an ever-present possibility in an Africa that was still largely uncivilized and without the medical advantages available in America.

The director decided to send Herbert and other young men ahead to Lake Albert on the Congo frontier where they would help build houses for the women missionaries. They traveled by train and then by truck. When they arrived at Lake Albert, a British steamboat took them across the lake, put them ashore and left them among the natives. A missionary named Fred Lanning came down from his mission station in Kasengu to meet them. He brought some of his mission boys and men to help carry the new arrivals' baggage on a four-hour walk up a rough, steep mountain trail to reach the station. When they arrived, they crowded into a row of mud and thatched dormitories that barely met their needs. Herbert's old Navy hammock, hung under the eaves of the mission house, provided his sleeping quarters. They all had to do their own cooking.

Herbert was good at learning languages and quickly learned Swahili, the language into which Dr. David Livingstone had translated the Bible. He was able, therefore, to talk with chiefs and headmen who knew the Swahili language. While helping build the mud and thatched houses for the women missionaries, Herbert also set about learning the Alur language, Dhu Alur, and within a few weeks made himself fairly well understood. Now he could share the Gospel in two African languages.

The mission director began to send out parties of two, four and five missionaries to different sites where they had decided to establish stations to work among the people. The director assigned Herbert and Jack Litchman, a converted Jew, to accompany Andy Uhlinger and his wife to open up a station among the Bahema and Babira people. Miss Ruth Fuller requested to go with them as the teacher in the mission school. She told the director that she had a "special reason" for wanting to go. Secretly she hoped that Herbert would take notice of her and that God would lead them to serve Him together. She had a good bicycle and went with the Uhlingers' caravan, composed of the missionaries on bicycles and native porters on foot, carrying the supplies.

Herbert, Jack and Director Lanning went later. It took five long days of hiking to reach their destination. Porters helped carry all the equipment and baggage. After passing through many big villages and the Kilo gold mines, at last they arrived at Bogoro. On a beautiful site overlooking Lake Albert, the men built, studied the language and preached. The women started a school for the native children and learned to cook and do household chores in their primitive surroundings. Within six months' time, the missionaries completed the frame of the Uhlingers' house, started a school and held regular meetings to preach God's Word.

Then the director sent Herbert and Jack to open another station among the Balendu people at Blukwa, high in the Balega Mountains. Because many of the tribes were at war, the men they hired from one tribe could carry the baggage only near the border of the next tribe. There they left the baggage and went back home. Herbert and Jack had to hunt and talk and pray to find porters from another tribe who would carry their baggage for the next leg of the trip. This method caused their expense for hiring porters to be more than they had planned. Jack and Herbert decided that Jack should go back the three days' journey to Djugu, the nearest government post, to get a load of small coins called "makutas" and "catawanjas" to pay the porters for the rest of the trip. Herbert would stay with the supplies.

While waiting for Jack to return, the porters became nervous and left Herbert alone on a bare hilltop with all the baggage. Herbert pleaded with them to stay, but to no avail. They walked away and left him standing by himself. He threw himself face down on the ground and prayed for God's help. After he finished praying, he heard footsteps and looked up to see a government headman dressed in the official khaki shirt and short pants.

"Have these savages gone off and left you again? I'll fix them," the man said. He shouldered his rifle, turned and marched away.

Again, Herbert was alone, wondering what God would do now. Soon the government official returned with enough porters to carry all of the baggage relay style to the village of the great Bahema chief, Blukwa, who ruled over both the Balendu and Bahema tribes. Jack was quite surprised to return a few days later and find Herbert and all their baggage missing. After much inquiry, he learned from a local tribesman what had happened and went to join Herbert.

Old Chief Blukwa received Herbert and Jack in a friendly way and invited them into his great round, grass house. The house was twenty feet high in the center and was about thirty feet in diameter. It had three partitions for his many wives. Chief Blukwa was of royal blood and he ruled his people with wisdom and power. He never looked directly at Herbert; instead, he turned his face sideways and glanced at him from the corner of his eyes. When he did so, it seemed as if his eyes flashed fire like a leopard's eyes. Herbert felt the chief was possessed of an evil spirit.

Herbert told the chief that they had come to tell his people about the great God in heaven who had sent his Son, Jesus Christ, to save them from their sins and take them to heaven when they died. He explained that they would build a school and teach the children how to read God's book. This seemed to please the chief. He promised to call all of the men to work for the missionaries and help them build the mission station. However, they found few of the men were really willing to work and progress was slow.

Compared to the Balendus, the Bahemas were a superior tribe. The Bahemas were considered rich because they owned many head of cattle and lived primarily by trading beef, milk and butter. The Balendus were an agricultural people, raising kaffir corn, millet, beans and sweet potatoes. They had many head of fat-tailed sheep and goats that they used mainly for buying wives.

The Bahema man would have to pay three or four head of cattle in order to buy a wife from his own tribe, yet he could buy a Balendu woman for only one cow. Therefore, many of the Bahema men bought Balendu women for wives. Since the children usually spoke the language of their mothers, the Bahema tribe became more like the Balendu tribe.

The two tribes were different in how they dressed. The Bahema women wore tanned and softened skins of cows or calves, with many strings of beads and shells. The men wore long, flowing "kanzus," yards of cloth draped over their shoulders and reaching down to their feet. They usually carried long spears. The Balendu women wore an abbreviated apron made of skins. They, too, wore numerous strands of beads, and painted their bodies and faces. The men wore tanned sheep or goatskin breechclouts, passed between the legs and supported at the waist by a fiber cord of rawhide strap. The women softened the skins by chewing on them for long hours. The men also painted their arms and legs with charcoal mixed with oil from the castor bean, grown for that purpose. They chiseled their teeth sharp like a dog's teeth and twisted their kinky hair into pigtails. They made cuts in their cheeks and foreheads, which left them marked with cicatrices (scars).

The men of both tribes always carried short bows and arrows with barbed iron heads. In wartime they carried tough, woven fiber shields and spears with a slender shaft attached through the end. When they threw the spear at an enemy, they let the shaft slide through their hand to the end and then drew it back quickly for another throw.

Herbert and Jack began to study the Batha (Balendu) language with the boys they had hired to carry water and firewood and to help with cooking. The language was not hard to learn or pronounce, but getting the order and construction of the words into sentences was difficult. The language was completely monosyllable. The five vowels were all words and each one had several meanings. Each vowel was used with each letter of the alphabet to form other words. Some words had no vowels at all. The sentence structure seemed awkward and backward to Herbert. "Yeso u na ke ka go nba" meant, "Jesus believing person will be saved yes." In English a person would say, "A person who believes in Jesus will be saved." Herbert would eventually learn to speak six African languages, though Batha was always his favorite.

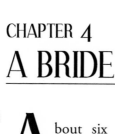

CHAPTER 4
A BRIDE

About six months after the Blukwa station was well established, the general director of the mission ordered Herbert to take over the Aru station on the Uganda border. No other missionaries were there. Herbert was alone with not even a cat for a companion. He became very lonely and discouraged.

One day as he was building a round table, he decided he would leave his station for a while and go back to British East Africa to find a wife among the missionary women there. He said to himself, "As soon as this table is finished, I will go to the village, hire porters to carry my baggage and start out."

He needed a vine to nail around the edge of the table. He went into the forest and found a big vine hanging straight down from a tree—just what he wanted! He climbed the tree and cut down the vine. When he climbed up the tree, no ants were in sight, but when he started down, hundreds of big pincher ants were coming up the tree to attack him. What a dilemma he faced! Pincher ants ranged in size from one to fifteen millimeters and traveled in columns—sometimes twelve inches wide and up to two hundred feet long. Herbert did not take time to guess how many were in this column. He only knew that their bite could be extremely painful and that if they attacked him, they would swarm all over him, and using some unknown communication system, they would all start biting at the same time. He quickly climbed back up the tree to escape. He could find nowhere else to go! His only option was to try crossing over to the next tree. He tried to jump across to the other tree as monkeys do, but his hands slipped and he fell about twenty-five feet, striking his right side on a stump and breaking a rib.

Herbert felt as if a knife were stabbing his side with each breath he took. He could only lie there gasping and groaning for about an hour. There was no one to come to his aid. Finally, he crawled back to his house and went to bed for four days, only painfully leaving his bed long enough to cook oatmeal porridge or anything else he had in the house to eat. Never in his life had he felt so alone and forsaken. In spite of his feelings of discouragement, however, he knew in his heart that God had not forsaken him, for Jesus had said, "I will never leave thee nor forsake thee." He also knew that the Lord had kept him from running away as Jonah had.

When the general director got word many weeks later of Herbert's accident and loneliness, he ordered him back to headquarters at Aba to help in his office for a while. Herbert wasn't happy there either. He tried to run away again but the porters he had hired told the general director. The director called Herbert to him and asked, "What is the big idea?"

"I am lonely living by myself and want to go to British East Africa to find a wife," Herbert confessed.

Kind, old, gray-headed Dr. Hurlburt put his arm around Herbert's shoulder and said, "Grings, the Lord wanted to give you a wife long ago, but you wouldn't take the hint. That schoolteacher at Bogoro, Miss Ruth Fuller, thinks the world of you."

Herbert had no idea! As he thought about it, however, he realized what a lovely, godly young woman Ruth Fuller was.

She had certainly proven her dedication to the Lord and to serving Him in Africa. She would make a wonderful wife. Why hadn't Herbert seen it before?

He immediately sat down and wrote Ruth a letter. Since no cars, planes or trains were available to carry the mail in that part of the Congo, the letter had to go by foot messengers and took three weeks to reach Ruth. It took another three weeks for her answer to reach Herbert. He thought those were the longest weeks of his life.

Finally, Ruth's answer arrived. She wrote, "Dear Boy: Oh, I have been waiting so long for this letter." She accepted Herbert's proposal. The Lord had a wife ready and waiting for him. He just needed to realize how much he needed her.

Herbert was so excited he could hardly wait to begin the ten-day safari from Aba to Bogoro. He hired porters to carry his baggage and made the other necessary preparations, including making sure his bicycle was in shape for the trip. As soon as possible, he started for Bogoro. He was in such a hurry that one day he rode far ahead of his porters and that night they did not catch up with him at the rest house where he stopped. He had to sleep on a bamboo table without a blanket or mosquito net. Myriads of malarial mosquitoes swarmed around him and he was cold, so he didn't sleep much that night. Because of his foolish haste, he suffered an attack of malarial fever, delaying him four days at the Ter Akara mission station. He learned the truth of the proverb he had learned as a child, "Haste makes waste."

At last he arrived at Bogoro. Now that he had a willing heart, he fell in love with Ruth and within a week's time, he and the young schoolteacher agreed to get married as soon as possible. They learned, however, that to get married in the Belgian Congo they would be required to wait a year in order to get all the legal documents. They did not want to wait that long, so "love found a way." They joined a big caravan that included a missionary bachelor as chaperon, and went over into Uganda. On December 3, 1919, the commissioner married Herbert and Ruth under British law.

The ceremony was brief. The district commissioner asked Herbert, "Will you have this woman for your wife?" Herbert replied, "I will."

The official turned to Ruth. "Will you have this man for your husband?"

"Yes, sir!"

The commissioner read the law that if they were ever divorced and married again, they would be guilty of adultery. The wedding was over. Herbert had a bride who would be his faithful companion and serve by his side as they endeavored to reach the people of Africa with the Good News of Jesus Christ.

CHAPTER 5
JILO, THE FIRST BELIEVER

Herbert and Ruth made the trip back to Aba by traveling mostly at night because of the high heat and humidity in the daytime. Even with bright moonlight, travel by night was more dangerous because the fiercest animals came out at night to hunt and feed. The sounds and smells of the night jungle with its thick, dense overgrowth could be terrifying. Many women would have been afraid to undertake such a journey, but Ruth had every confidence that God would keep them safe. She knew she and Herbert were living in God's will and He would protect those who did so.

They rode their bicycles leisurely along ahead of their porters and cook boys. Once they passed through a country where wild buffaloes, one of the most dangerous animals, wandered about at night. Another time they had to walk and push or carry their bicycles over hundreds of holes in the path. Elephants weighing two tons or more had evidently passed that way not long before, and their feet had made deep impressions in the ground. They did not see leopards although they could sense their presence.

After they arrived back at Aba, the general director assigned Herbert and Ruth to open a new station at Linga, which was one long day's journey over thirteen ridges and ravines. They hired porters to carry their few belongings and began their journey on their bicycles. They arrived at the government official's plantation where the people received and treated them as guests.

A few days later, Herbert left Ruth at the plantation while he went to explore the Balendu tribe territory. He told Ruth, "If I find two large villages within a day's walking distance of each other, I will consider that the Lord's place for us."

Herbert came back after several days to report that he had found not two but five big villages averaging three hundred people each, with a splendid station site about midway among them and a little way off the government road. The headman of the Linga village had invited him to come and live among his people. Herbert and Ruth hastened to move to the village. Herbert secured porters to carry Ruth in a "tipoi," which is a chair swung on bamboo poles, as well as their entire household goods and baggage.

When they arrived at the village a great crowd of nearly naked men, women and children met them, wearing only loincloths or aprons. The natives had never seen a white woman before. Ruth now spoke three African languages and Herbert spoke four. They talked to the people and with the help of an intelligent headman as interpreter, Herbert preached the Gospel of Christ to them.

They camped in the government rest house not far from the village while Herbert went every day to clear the station site and build a house. Because not many men wanted to work for him at first, he built just one round mud and wattle house that was fifteen feet in diameter with one door and two windows. Although the red mud in the walls was not yet dry when he and Ruth moved in, the little house was their own home and they were as happy as any love birds in their nests could be. They had to do their cooking on an open fire outside. Ruth put her shining pots into the fire, never to see them shine again.

The witch doctor opposed Herbert and Ruth, warning the young boys not to work for them or attend their school. He started a rumor that the missionaries had a hole under their table and if a boy bringing them food from the outside fireplace came near, they would grab him, throw him into the hole and then eat him. Since some of the tribes in the area practiced cannibalism, this rumor was not hard for the people to believe. Therefore, at first Herbert and Ruth had to cut their own firewood and carry their water from the spring in the ravine.

One day a young man named Jilo came to the door and said he wanted to work for them. Herbert gladly gave him a machete and hoe, and told him to clear the path to the water spring. Jilo worked diligently for two or three hours and came back saying he had cleared the path. Herbert inspected Jilo's work and found it to be very satisfactory. Herbert then tried to tell him how God created the world, but Jilo seemed nervous and asked for his pay so he could go to the village and buy something to eat. Herbert gave him a catawanja, which was a coin with a hole in the center. The Balendus delighted to put these coins on a string and tie them about their waists or necks. Jilo took the money and went away quickly.

The next day Jilo came back, worked and got another catawanja. This time he listened a little better to the Bible story Herbert told him, though he hurried away to the village as soon as Herbert would let him go. He came back the third and fourth days and worked, bringing poles and thatch grass for a little cookhouse Herbert was building. On the fifth day Herbert finished the cookhouse, and that day Jilo listened intently to the story of Jesus opening the eyes of the blind man. After the story, Herbert persuaded Jilo to kneel with him as he talked to the invisible Lord Jesus for him. Then he asked Jilo if he would like to make his bed in the new cookhouse and stay with him and Ruth all the time. Jilo fearfully accepted.

Since Ruth knew the Bahema language, she conversed with Jilo in it. This delighted Jilo and seemed to relieve his fear of Herbert and Ruth. Little by little they learned that Jilo was the son of the sub-chief who lived down by the lake near the mountains. His father was Bahema and his mother was Balendu. He said he was to inherit the chieftainship when his old father died, but his brothers were jealous of him and threatened to kill him.

Jilo had heard of the "muzungu" (white man) at Linga, and he had been told that the muzungu bewitched and killed people. Although he was very curious and wanted to see the white man, he was afraid he would die if he did. Still he was more afraid of dying at the hands of his brothers, so he decided to take the risk and found his way to the mission station. After working for Herbert the first day, he went to the village and spent the night fearfully, expecting some terrible thing to happen to him, but nothing happened. He went the second, third and fourth days, and still no calamity occurred. Now he was willing to stay and be their cook boy.

Day by day, Ruth taught Jilo Bible stories in his native language. He was an eager learner. Then one day he knelt down with Herbert and Ruth and gave his heart to the Lord Jesus. He was the first person to trust the Savior under their ministry in Africa. It was hard to tell who was happier—Jilo or Herbert and Ruth! He eagerly learned the "Words of God." Soon he began using his influence to bring other boys from the village to work for them, to attend the school and to hear the stories from the Bible.

After Jilo had worked for the Gringses about three months, he went to Herbert and said, "Teacher, I want to go back to my village down by the lake and bring my brothers here to learn the words of God."

Herbert and Ruth were concerned about what might happen to him, but after prayer and counsel, they sent him away. They wondered about his safety and prayed for him every day. He was gone about ten days. When he returned, he brought two of his younger brothers who had earlier threatened to kill him. Before long, they too, received the Savior. Soon boys and girls, and men and women began coming to the meetings from villages far and near. Many put their faith in Jesus Christ! The school attendance also increased greatly. Herbert and Ruth humbly thanked God for opening the spiritual eyes of the Bahema and Balendu people.

CHAPTER 6

FROM PLACE TO PLACE

Because the people of the villages had great medical needs, the mission headquarters decided to send a doctor and his family to take over the work at the Linga station and send Herbert and Ruth to open a new station among the Alur and Bakebu tribes. They opened the new station near the village of Kbandro-ma, a name that meant, "they hate me." Later the station was called "Rethy" after the name of the low flat-topped hill on which it was built. The men from these villages were more willing to work than the people of the Linga village were, and they helped Herbert build a rather comfortable, three-room mud and wattle house where he and Ruth could live. They had no money to pay the workmen, so Ruth made "ru-mbi" (cloth string girdles) to give the men for pay. They also used empty food tin cans, needles, safety pins, and similar small items to pay the workers and to trade for food supplies. The mission treasurer sent them a check; however, there was no place to cash it in the jungles and they had to return it.

The house had no wooden doors, only drop mats woven from the elephant grass, and rats infested the house. Herbert set traps for them. When he heard the trap go "snap" in the night Herbert got up, took the dead rat out of the trap, threw it outside of the door, set the trap again and went back to bed.

In the morning, he looked for the dead rat outside the door but it was not there. The next night after a rainstorm, he threw another dead rat outside the door and went back to bed. When he looked for it in the morning, he did not find it; instead, there in the mud just in front of the door were large leopard tracks! Herbert hurried to get something more substantial than a drop mat to close the door. Never again did he throw rats out in front of the door!

While at the Kba-ndro-ma (Rethy) station, the Gringses received a special gift from God, their first son. Herbert and Ruth made the trip back to Linga for the baby to be born so that a medical doctor would be available for the delivery. While they were all awaiting the birth of the baby, a call came asking Dr. Trout to go to Lake Albert where a Belgian Government official lay gravely ill with the black-water fever. This would be a safari of five or six days to go and return. What should Dr. Trout do? The Lord seemed to impress on his heart that a missionary's wife who could teach school and the Word of God in four native languages had priority over a government official. However, he could not ignore the man completely. He sent Herbert with medications and instructions for treating the official.

Herbert rode his bicycle as far and as fast as he could go with it. Then he traveled seven thousand feet down the escarpment on foot. From there he got the government soldiers to help him secure porters who carried him by night in a tipoi to where the government official lay dying. At that time, black-water fever, which was a serious, complicated form of malaria, was fatal in nine out of ten cases. Herbert administered the medications according to Dr. Trout's instructions. He then received word that a doctor from another station was coming to treat the official. Herbert was free to make the exhausting trip back to his wife, hoping all the while that he would be there in time for the baby's birth. He was relieved to find he had arrived in time. He and Ruth welcomed their first child, Robert Ernest, into the world and their hearts on November 15, 1920. They could not know at that time what a great blessing he would be in their ministry and in the future evangelism of Africa.

After Ruth recovered her strength, they returned to their own station. Soon after Robert was born, the mission sent them back to the Linga station. From there they rode their bicycles out into the surrounding villages, carrying Robert in a sling on Ruth's back. Sometimes they went out with a tent, and preached and taught for weeks at a time in the villages. The baby was a great attraction to the natives, who had never seen a white woman and her child. Ruth and Robert always attracted a crowd. Sometimes Herbert would preach ten or fifteen times a day, beginning at dawn and ending by moonlight.

When another missionary died, Herbert and Ruth went to the Blukwa station. Before they moved, however, they visited the mission hospital at Rethy where their second son, Roy Gerald, was born. He, too, would help reach the people of Africa with the Gospel.

Using local material, the former missionary at the Blukwa station had built a nice house with a Swedish touch. Having a more secure and comfortable home, with its wooden doors and window shutters, was wonderful. Ruth was especially thrilled that it had a kitchen with an iron stove. She no longer had to cook outside on firestones. Both Herbert and Ruth were determined, however, not to let these comforts keep them tied down to the station.

Herbert went out for two weeks on preaching trips to the surrounding villages. When he got back, Ruth would say, "Now it's my turn." She would take the baby and leave Robert with

Herbert. Two of the schoolboys went with Ruth and carried baby Roy in a basket tied to a pole. They would be gone for a week or more while Ruth taught the women and children in the villages.

God blessed their ministry. Both the school and the preaching services increased greatly in attendance. The Sunday morning services grew from sixty or seventy to five hundred and then to one thousand. People began gathering before seven o'clock in the morning to listen to the preaching of the Word of God, although most had to stand outside the building.

Herbert trained five of the young men to go out and preach the Gospel. They walked to distant villages. Those who opposed the Gospel ridiculed them and called them "Tze-jo-nga-bi-na-kba," which means "ridge walkers." When they told Herbert how the villagers treated them, he reminded them of something he had learned as a child, "Well, we have to suffer persecution if we want to serve the Lord."

The young men faithfully gave out the Gospel message in the villages despite opposition and, sometimes, persecution. Before long, some of the people listened and believed. Soon the young evangelists began bringing people from the villages to the station for Sunday morning services.

During this time, a third child was born to Herbert and Ruth. They were blessed with a daughter, whom they named Elisabeth and called Bessie. They went to the mission hospital for Bessie to be born. When they started home, they couldn't find enough porters to carry the tipoi for Ruth. She wrapped the baby in a cloth slung around her neck and rode her bicycle. Herbert carried Robert and Roy on his bicycle. Crowds of people in every village they passed through wanted to see the baby. Ruth witnessed to more women on that trip than any before.

The people greatly loved Ruth and fondly called her "Mama." She found just caring for her own family an extremely difficult task in such primitive conditions.

Much of their clothing was "hand-made" or "made-over." Meals were all "from scratch" and composed of native products gleaned from the forest or purchased from the natives and cooked on primitive stoves. Clothing was all washed by hand and seldom seemed to dry completely in a land where the rains were heavy nine to ten months of the year and where it was damp and humid even when it did not rain. Ruth gave untiringly of herself both to her family and to the African people. She thoroughly educated her own children and taught them to read at a very early age. She instilled Biblical principles in their lives and insisted upon faithful Scripture memorization. She also taught the native people to read, taught them God's Word and ministered to their physical needs in many ways. She even played fireman!

One day as Herbert was coming back from a preaching trip and was yet some distance away, he noticed smoke rising above the village. When he arrived at the station, he learned that while the native women stood around screaming and wailing, Ruth ran into a burning house and dragged out a boy whom lightning had stunned, and who could not escape from the fiery house. Because of her faith and courage, the people greatly respected her.

The Gringses now had as many as one-hundred and fifty young men on their pay roll. They never asked for funds from anyone to feed or pay the young men, and they never went in debt. God always supplied their needs. With so many people living at the mission station, they necessarily raised part of their food. Besides planting beans and corn, the principal diet of the natives, Herbert brought in red and French blue potatoes and began planting them. The natives soon learned to like this new food and carried potato seed to their own villages for their families to plant.

When Jack and Herbert first opened this mission station upon arriving in Africa, they planted black wattle trees that grew from seed. As the trees grew, they beautified the station and furnished an abundance of seed that the natives carried to other villages and planted. Thus, groves of beautiful trees began springing up on many of the ridges where the villages were located.

CHAPTER 7
SAVED BY JESUS' NAME

When the Belgian Government officials came to the Congo, they wanted the natives to pay taxes. Sometimes the people refused and they used poisoned arrows to shoot the black soldiers who came to collect the taxes. The soldiers retaliated by shooting men, women and children with their rifles.

One sub-chief revolted and took his people over the mountain to live by the lake on the other side, thinking they could get away from the government. The government official sent word to him that if he did not return and build his village beside the government road, his soldiers would come and make war on them.

When Herbert heard what the government official had done, he said to Ruth, "If he goes down there he will kill a lot of people. I believe God wants me to go first and preach to the people."

Ruth agreed and they committed the matter to the Lord in prayer. Herbert took five schoolboys to carry his folding cot, chop box and tent, and they started over the mountain to the rebel village. Herbert did not take a gun, for he never carried one. A year or so later some believers from that village told him that not having a gun had probably saved his life that day.

They told him, "Teacher, when you passed through the forest we were hiding behind trees ready to shoot with our poisoned arrows but when we looked out and saw no soldiers and no gun, just a lone white man with those young men, we said, 'What kind of white man is that? Let him go.'"

They allowed Herbert to pass safely over the mountain and down the other side. The rebel village stood on a ridge below. Some of the people looking up and seeing Herbert's white sun helmet thought he was the government official coming to make war with them. Suddenly there was a commotion in the village. The boys drove off the sheep and goats while the women grabbed their pots and young children and fled to the forest. The men set fire to their grass huts and scattered to the forest preparing to fight to the finish. Herbert did not fully realize the danger, but the boys with him understood and they lined up behind him.

Herbert ran through the clearing shouting, "Don't burn your houses! Don't burn your houses!"

Just then he saw a man crouching behind a log with the arrow drawn taut on his bow. Herbert stood still, expecting to feel the arrow pierce his body. Instead, the Holy Spirit whispered in his heart, "Tell him, 'Don't kill me, I am a man of Jesus.'"

Herbert raised his hands above his head and shouted, "Nzi hwi ma hwi. Ma ku Yesu dza ke!"

The man had probably never heard the name of Jesus before yet when he heard the words "Yesu dza ke," he lowered his bow and arrow. Herbert slowly approached the man and said, "Don't fight against the government official. He has guns that can shoot five times. He can kill all of you. Call the people. I want to tell you the words of Jesus."

The warrior pressed his cheeks together with his thumb and middle finger and cried "Ho-o-o-o-lo," ending the "lo" by snapping his thumb and middle finger sharply through his open mouth. The other warriors, armed with bows and arrows and spears, responded to his call and surrounded Herbert. They were painted and tattooed; they had chiseled their teeth as sharp as a dog's teeth; they had charcoal rubbed into their hair and wore goatskins for a loincloth.

Herbert explained to them, "I am not a government official but a Jesus man. I have not come to make war; I have come to tell you the words of God."

The people sat down by the burning embers of their houses, now completely consumed by the fire. The women and children came back from hiding; everyone sat for hours as Herbert told them the words of God.

When Herbert told the natives about Abel's blood sacrifice they said, "We understand because we give blood sacrifices to GO."

"Who is GO?" Herbert asked. "Is he a good spirit?"

"Go Ku che (Satan is bad)," they said.

Herbert asked, "What is the name of the good God who made the earth and sky and sun and moon and all things?"

The young men hesitated to speak his name but finally, after some questioning, an old man answered, "Ke ro tho ku JA." (His name is JA.) That was the Hebrew name for Jehovah. Sometime in their history, the ancestors of these people had heard about the true God and God had preserved His name in that heathen tribe!

That night Herbert slept in his tent and the people slept around the open fires. The next morning he preached to them again, urging them to submit to the government official by returning and building their village beside the government road. He said that if they would do so and build a schoolhouse, he would send someone to teach them the words of God. They agreed. Herbert went home and told Ruth how close she had come to being a widow!

Within two weeks the rebels submitted to the government. They built their village where the official ordered and built a schoolhouse. Herbert sent one of the most capable married couples from another mission station to teach them. Soon many of the people trusted Jesus as their Savior. The Gospel changed not only their hearts but also their ways of living. Before long the goatskin breechclouts and grass aprons gave way to pants, shirts and dresses.

The white men came, discovered gold in the little streams and hired the natives to work the mines. Traders arrived with all sorts of European and Asiatic products for sale. Aluminum pots, cups and dishes replaced the earthen pots, gourds and calabashes. With the introduction of the Gospel, a new era dawned for the Balendu people.

CHAPTER 8
DREARY WANDERINGS

After eight years of constant, faithful service in the Belgian Congo, the mission board decided to send Herbert and Ruth back to America. They sadly said goodbye to the native believers and prepared to leave. They had a delay of two months at Kijabe in British East Africa while they awaited the birth of their fourth child, Grant Fuller. Herbert was not idle during this time, though. While they waited, Herbert copied his translations of the Gospels of Mark and Luke, and sent them to the Congo.

The Grings family received no funds at all from the mission board for their passage to America. To help raise their passage, other missionaries provided funds from their own support money. The amount raised was only sufficient for Herbert and his family to be deck passengers on the ship. This meant they had to sleep on deck and had to bring all of their own food and supplies for the journey.

The grocery man was supposed to send a case of milk for the baby with the other groceries. When baby Grant was hungry, Herbert went to their supplies to find a tin of milk for him. He searched in vain for the case of milk. Apparently, the grocer had neglected to include it with the other supplies. They had a seventeen-day ocean voyage ahead and no milk for the baby. What would they do? Herbert later said, "If ever I was tempted to doubt the goodness of the Lord, it was then."

Instead of letting his doubt conquer his faith, however, he went into a corner, knelt down and prayed, "Lord, forgive me for doubting you. I don't understand, still I will trust you— even if the baby dies."

Ruth found a big bottle of malted milk (such as convalescent patients may drink) and two tins of milk in the chop box. They used this for the baby instead of allowing the other children to have milk on their porridge. Before the voyage ended, they persuaded the ship's steward to give them some canned milk from the first class section of the ship. They had enough to last until they put in port at Singapore. The baby thrived on it!

From Singapore to Kobe, Japan, the weather was too cold for the family to go as deck passengers. The steward put them into a compartment in second class with other poor passengers. The situation was not comfortable or pleasant. The ship put ashore for some weeks at Kobe, because of the weather. Herbert immediately sought a place to stay. Right away, he saw a sign in English in front of a real estate office. Upon entering the office, he found the agent spoke very good English. Herbert inquired about lodging in the area and learned that the man had a big, unfurnished, upstairs room in a house near the dock. Herbert rented it and brought Ruth, the children and all their baggage ashore. They happily cooked their food and slept on the floor instead of going to an expensive hotel.

Herbert did not waste time even during this delay. Finding that printing was very cheap at Kobe, he engaged a printer and had five hundred copies of a little book of Old Testament stories printed in the Batha language. These he sent to the Congo for the other missionaries to use in teaching the native people. The Batha people were eager to learn to read so they could have their own "Words of God."

When the Grings family left Japan, they again took third class passage in a deck compartment with immigrants and poor people. When the ship stopped at Honolulu, Hawaii, some missionaries came aboard to visit them. These missionaries lovingly paid the difference in passage cost and put the Grings family in a big, comfortable, second class cabin for the rough and tempestuous voyage on to San Francisco.

Herbert later called the family's wanderings in America a "long and drab story." They bought an old Chevy truck and a trailer for baggage and went to Arizona, hoping to find Indians among whom they could do missionary work. They were disappointed when this did not work out, but they sought God's direction concerning where to go next. Herbert's two stepbrothers offered him a job in their car agency in North Dakota. He took Bobby with him and headed there to work while Ruth took the rest of the children and went to visit her sister in Ohio. The family was not happy being apart.

A Christian college in Florida invited Herbert to work in their office. Ruth and the children rejoined him and they headed for Florida. After laboring there for several months, Herbert resigned and gave himself completely to translating and typing the manuscript of the New Testament in Batha. He sent it to Blukwa where the language committee of the Africa Inland Mission revised it and had it printed in London. This project was Herbert's final work for the Balendu tribe.

In 1928, Herbert and Ruth's daughter Louise was born. With a wife and five children to support and the Batha New Testament completed, Herbert needed to find employment. He passed the civil service exam and accepted an assignment to the Lake City Veterans Administration Hospital in Lake

City, Florida. A new door of service for the Lord also opened. Herbert went to churches to show his African pictures and Bible slides with a projector. He lectured on missions in churches and schoolhouses, and preached in churches. On Sundays, Ruth and the children accompanied him to help in the Sunday schools. He was soon preaching twice every Sunday and showing his pictures almost every weeknight. He wanted to help American Christians understand both the need for more Christians to go to the mission fields and the necessity to help support those who went. Herbert paid all of his own living and travel expenses, receiving no money for his services.

Herbert found an abandoned Baptist church that he reopened and pastored for a while. He soon had a strong Sunday school going, a preaching service in the morning and his stereopticon Bible lectures at night. When the church was doing well again, however, the former pastor came back and said the church was his. Herbert graciously stepped down and let the old pastor run the meetings. He and Ruth stayed and helped with the Sunday school.

During a thirty-day leave with pay from his job at the hospital, Herbert and Ruth decided to take the family and drive up to Greenville, North Carolina, to spend the time at a Christian life conference. The conference was a great blessing and encouragement to them. During the trip, the Grings family camped in a tourist camp swarming with mosquitoes. In Africa they were always careful to sleep under nets, but in the United States they thought they were not in danger. A few days after they arrived home, little Grant became very ill with a fever. The doctor diagnosed a severe form of malaria and immediately hospitalized him. Help had come too late, though. He died that afternoon, and his family buried him the next day.

Herbert and Ruth were heartbroken, but God's sustaining

grace enabled them to settle back into life. Herbert worked and preached; Ruth stayed busy with the other children and continued to help her husband. Herbert felt he needed a change after Grant's death and moved his family to Tampa, Florida. There he secured a job with the Prohibition Border Patrol. The job lasted briefly because some of the ungodly patrol officers resented Herbert's outspoken testimony for Christ and managed to get him fired. The family moved back to Lake City and Herbert returned to work at Veterans Hospital. He also continued to hold meetings in churches. At this time his mother came to live with the family for a while.

One night during this time, Herbert took his family to a meeting he was holding in a little country church. Since they had gotten an early start, Herbert decided to drive by a bootlegger's house to invite him and his family to the meeting. It was starting to get dark. As Herbert turned a corner, he could see a light in the house, then suddenly it went off. He drove the car up to the front gate and waited for someone to come out, but no one did. The house and the porch were completely dark, so Herbert decided no one was home and turned the car around to leave. As he did, he heard a loud bang, which sounded like a gunshot.

Herbert swung the car in front of the house across from the bootlegger's house, where the man's parents lived. The old man opened the door a wee bit in the glare of the car's headlights and hollered, "Who's doin' that shootin'?"

"It's not me; it's that fellow over there," said Herbert.

The old man slammed the door shut. Somehow, Herbert knew that was not a good sign. He turned his lights off and stepped on the gas to get away quickly. Bang! Bang! Someone fired the gun. Herbert felt a shot whiz by the car window, though by then he was far enough away that he was out of harm's reach.

When they arrived at the church, Herbert sent his family into the building. He got his flashlight and examined the car. He found a hole and a pistol bullet that had lodged in the spring cushion where his mother had been sitting. If it had been two inches higher, it would have entered her back and probably killed her. Little Louise had been sitting in the back seat behind her grandmother, her legs in line with the path of the bullet. However, she had moved over just before the bootlegger had fired.

The next day Herbert drove back to the bootlegger's house and showed him the hole in the car. The man's wife said he had thought Herbert was a police officer, coming to arrest him for making illegal "booze" and had come out on the porch and fired the pistol at him. She had pulled his hand down just as he shot, causing him to miss. Herbert witnessed to the man and tried to persuade him to turn to the Lord for salvation, but he refused. Herbert drove away, saddened by the man's rejection of the Savior yet praising God for the protection He had given his family.

In 1931 Herbert and Ruth's sixth child, Mark, was born. The same year the great depression hit the United States and Herbert lost his job. He had not been content in the U.S. and longed to be serving the Lord in Africa, so when he lost his job, he said to Ruth, "This is just the Lord giving us a push to go back to Africa."

Ruth agreed. She, too, desired to be back on the mission field. With no mission board to back them and no promise of financial support from anyone, they set their faces for the Congo.

Their first challenge was to obtain a visa to reenter the country. This was a problem because they no longer had the sponsorship of a mission board. However, they got two missionaries in the Congo to write letters of recommendation for them, which enabled them to receive their visas. The next challenge was to find passage. They did not have enough money to sail by passenger steam ship.

One evening Herbert closed one of his lectures on Africa by projecting a beautiful picture of a sailing ship on a screen. He sang a song that had these words: "Far across the deep blue ocean in a dark and dreary land, a million souls in darkness are dying fast on every hand. They never heard the story of how the Savior died, nor of the Roman soldier who pierced his side. If you'll just send me across the deep blue sea, I'll tell them of my Savior and of how he died for me. I'll tell the story to them, if you'll just send me."

At the close of the service someone said to Herbert, "Why don't you go on that old sailing ship at Fernandina sea port?"

Early the next day he went to Fernandina and found a big, four-masted schooner, the Augusta G. Hilton. She was due to sail in a few days for Cape Verde Islands, just off the west coast of Africa. From there the Gringses could get a steam ship to the Congo. Herbert told the captain they were missionaries and asked if he would grant them passage on the ship. The captain said he could not take them as passengers though they could sign on as crew if they would also pay eight hundred dollars. Herbert agreed and they signed on as "crew."

The holds of the ship had plenty of room and the family received permission to take as much baggage as they wanted. Herbert spent about a week buying what they needed, including medical supplies, school and printing supplies and personal belongings. He loaded fifty-three cases of goods and then put his car and trailer in the hold. To Herbert, though, the most valuable pieces of equipment in his outfit were his camera and his projector with the twelve hundred slides of Bible pictures that he intended to use for teaching the Bible to the natives.

At last, the Coast Guard tug towed the ship out of the harbor into the Atlantic Ocean. The crew hoisted the sails and the Gringses were on their way back to the Congo, the place of their hearts' desire.

CHAPTER 9
ABANDON SHIP!

The captain gave up his big, comfortable cabin to Ruth, the girls and little Mark. Herbert and the other two boys shared another small cabin. Herbert and Ruth brought extra provisions that they could add to the ship's fare so the children would have sufficient food.

Although The Hilton was an American built ship, two Portuguese manned her as captains. The first mate and eight of the crewmen, however, were black men. One crewman had his wife and baby with him. Ruth was glad not to be the only woman on board the ship. They all spoke English as well as Portuguese, which was a blessing for the Grings family because they were able to communicate with them as well as share the Gospel with them.

At first the wind was moderate but the Gulf Stream off the Atlantic coast was choppy as usual. The ship rolled and pitched considerably, ripping the sails, which the crew had to lower for repairs, causing hours of delay. The captain set course toward the Bermuda Islands in order to catch trade winds that would waft them across the ocean to the Cape Verde Islands. After three days' sailing, the old ship began to leak water so badly that they had to put in to the Bermuda Islands for repairs. This delay was in God's plan, for while there the Gringses made friends with some Portuguese Christians who later helped support them in the Congo. A diver went under the ship and patched the leak in the bottom of the hull. When they embarked again the captain took on thirty-one Portuguese passengers going back to Portugal by way of the Canary Islands.

Things went smoothly for about a week and in between their crew duties, Herbert, Ruth and the boys studied the Kikongo-Commercial language. However, the ship did not strike the trade winds as expected and there was not enough wind to fill the sails. Movement was slow. Then the ship began to leak again. The freshwater reserve tank also sprang a leak and all the fresh water leaked out into the bilges. No spare fresh water was available for steam to work the injection pump. The crew had to man the hand pump and bail the water out with buckets. Because the men had not received their wages and did not want to work, they broke the hand pump, leaving no way to pump the water out of the ship.

As the water continued to rise in the hold, the old ship began listing to starboard. If the cargo of lumber floated and shifted, the ship was in danger of capsizing. The captain estimated that they were about eight hundred miles from the nearest land. The ship had no radio so the captain could not call for help. The Grings family prayed for God to send a ship to rescue them.

Herbert showed his slides and preached to the passengers and crew twice a week. The last message he had preached was from the book of Acts on Paul's shipwreck. That night he took his projector up on the roof of the after cabin and flashed its bright beam in all directions, hoping another ship would spot it, but he received no answering signal from another ship.

The next morning the captain ordered everyone to prepare to abandon the ship. The crew lowered the big steel lifeboat and the little wooden ship-to-shore boat into the sea. Herbert also urged the crew to make two rafts from hatch covers and lower them. The Portuguese passengers began putting so much baggage into the big lifeboat that Herbert protested, fearing it would sink. No one else thought of taking fresh water and Herbert had a difficult time persuading a man to help him fill two small barrels with water and hoist them over the side of the ship into the lifeboats.

About noon, August 18, 1933, the captain gave the order, "Everybody in the lifeboats."

Herbert brought his family on deck and they all tied on their life belts. He turned to Robert and asked, "Bob, are you afraid to die?"

Bob answered, "No, Daddy, I'm trusting Jesus."

They, along with the second captain, six of the crew and a young Portuguese man from Bermuda, climbed down rope ladders into the little ship-to-shore boat. The boat was so heavily loaded that it rode very low in the water, with the deck only about twelve inches above the waterline. Herbert thanked the Lord that the sea was calm and the sun was shining brightly.

As soon as everyone was safely away from the ship, the captain had kerosene poured in the cabins and set the ship on fire to make a smoke signal for other ships to see and come to the rescue. What a test of Herbert and Ruth's faith it was to sit in the lifeboat and watch all of their outfit—automobile and trailer, four bicycles, medical and school supplies, printing press, sewing machine, personal goods and Herbert's precious projector and twelve hundred slides—burning up! Still God gave them an inward peace and confidence that everything was for their good. They still had an all wise, all knowing God who would be their refuge and help.

About four o'clock in the afternoon a storm blew up. Clouds as black as night seemed to merge with the ocean. The Grings family prayed and the Lord held back the rain. Not a drop fell on them, though the sea rose in great swells and water splashed into the little boat. The little wooden boat had no watertight compartments like the big steel lifeboat. It would sink with the first big wave! Some of the people panicked, fearing that death was certainly not far off, yet the Lord gave Herbert, Ruth and the children calmness.

Suddenly, the seamen shouted, "STEAMER!" The Dutch freighter Hercules quickly came alongside and dropped a sea ladder. The Grings family and the crew climbed aboard. The first thing the Gringses did was to sit down, and give thanks and praise to God for saving them. The freighter soon picked up the other groups. Fifteen minutes later the storm broke and rain and wind whipped the sea into raging white caps.

The captain of the Hercules, Captain Zindler, said that surely God had sent him with his ship to rescue them from that part of the Atlantic Ocean, which was outside the shipping lanes. He accounted that the day before, at the same hour that the Grings family prayed for God to send a rescue ship, a storm beat so violently on the bow of his ship that he had to change his course, which brought him directly to the spot of the sinking ship at just the moment most needed.

That night Captain Zindler had his radio operator send out a general call for ships to be on the lookout for the burnt hulk of the Hilton. He received no answer to his call. Apparently, there were no other ships in that entire region! God had heard the call of his faithful servants and sent the ship at just the right time to keep them from drowning.

One of the officers vacated his room for the Grings family. Ruth and the girls slept cuddled together in the bunk. Herbert and the boys slept on the floor. Food had to be limited because the Hercules did not have provisions for so great an emergency.

That night Herbert had a meeting on deck to give thanks and praise to God for saving them. Captain Zindler and his officers and all the crew who were not on duty attended. So did all the Portuguese.

Four days later, after twenty-nine days at sea, they sighted land. The captain had decided to take them to the high green mountains of Puerto Rico. Never had land looked so good to Herbert, Ruth and the children!

CHAPTER 10
CHRISTMAS AT HOME IN THE CONGO

The Grings family went ashore with one bag of clothing that they had been able to save and take in the lifeboat with them. They had to split up for housing, with Ruth, the girls and Mark staying with Methodist missionaries, and Herbert, Bob and Roy staying at the Y.M.C.A. During this time Ruth became so discouraged she wanted to go back to Florida.

"No," said Herbert. "That is just the devil trying to keep the Gospel from Africa. We still have some money and the Methodist missionaries have given us clothing; let's go without any outfit."

After praying over the matter together, Ruth agreed to go on. Herbert hurried to get a visa and booked passage on a big Spanish passenger ship going to Spain by way of the Canaries. From the Canary Islands they could take a ship to the Belgian Congo. Herbert dreaded having to take his family down into the crowded, third-class compartment because he could not afford better accommodations. When one of the ship's stewards asked for Herbert's passport, he took it and went to the purser's office. Soon the steward came back and beckoned Herbert and the family to come with him. He directed them to a nice cabin with six bunks and forced-air ventilation, located in second class—without extra charge. God had again graciously provided for his servants.

When they reached the Canary Islands, they met much opposition in trying to get passage to the Belgian Congo. The shipping agent kept denying them passage. Finally, one night, after seeing a ship in the harbor, Herbert said to Ruth, "We are going on that ship tonight."

Soon after dark, they took what little baggage they had gathered and went down to the landing. The ship's small boat was there just as if someone had sent it for them. Herbert asked the boatman if he would take them to the ship and he readily consented. When they came alongside the gangway, no one came to stop them, so they climbed up on deck. The purser came out and asked what they wanted. Herbert told him they wanted to go to the Belgian Congo. The purser asked to see their passport and said, "Do you have money for when you arrive in the Congo?"

Herbert showed him both their passport and his money. The purser made out a ticket for them, and gave orders to place them in a big second class cabin with all the comforts they needed. They even had a special table and waiter for meals. They were as well off as if they were wealthy passengers traveling in first class!

After twelve days, they disembarked at Point Noire in French Equatorial Africa. Another missionary took them in and cared for them until they could get passage on the railroad that was being constructed to Brazzaville. Missionaries at Brazzaville helped them get across Stanley Pool to Leopoldville. They were back in the Belgian Congo once more. How they praised God!

The Gringses began to understand why God had permitted their entire outfit to sink in the ocean. He wanted them to move lightly and rapidly. With that big outfit, they never could have gone very far from the river back into the dense jungles. They would have had to settle down on the riverbank and try to get the natives to come to them.

Herbert said, "God permitted the material things to be taken away from us so we would trust in spiritual things."

They bought some second hand household goods left by missionaries going on furlough. They had all that was necessary and felt confident God would supply anything else they would need.

From Leopoldville they went by river steamer to Kikwit and then by truck to Idiofa, and finally, by bicycle and porters and carrying chairs through a rain storm to Tshene, the mission station of old friends, the Anton Andersons. After a few days of fellowship, the Andersons helped them raise a caravan of porters and they started out to find a tribe needing evangelization, where they could open a new mission station.

Finally, they came to the Kasai River and Herbert went by canoe to make contact with some men of the large Bankutu tribe. The men wore fiber skirts and painted their bodies. They had leopard and crocodile teeth and other fetishes about their necks much like the Balendu people among whom the Gringses had worked in east Congo. They understood the Lingala language that Herbert knew. He explained to them who he was and what he wanted to do in their tribe. They readily agreed and said they would come and carry the family back into the forest to their village.

When Herbert went back and told Ruth, she was enthusiastic to enter the tribe. They crossed the crocodile infested Kasai River with their baggage and equipment in three "tippy" canoes and found the Bankutu men waiting for them. They had three bicycles. Ruth took little Mark on her bicycle and Herbert took

Bessie and Louise on his. Bob and Roy rode their one bicycle in relays. The porters followed.

That night they put up their camp cots in a small government rest house in the first village. The next morning was Christmas 1933. The children sat up in bed and excitedly opened what small presents Herbert and Ruth had been able to get for them while the native boys and girls, men and women looked in at the open front and side of the rest house. Herbert and Ruth realized that privacy was once more a thing of the past. Herbert told the people the Christmas story and preached to them in Lingala. The headman interpreted the message into the Bankuto language. Never had Christmas been so special!

CHAPTER 11
A NEW HOME

They stayed in the village about a week. Ruth made friends with the Bankut women and the children with their children. They needed, however, to learn more about the Bankutu people and find a more central location for their mission station. One day Herbert went on a day's bicycle ride through the forest to the government post at Oshwe on the Lukenia River. The government officials were surprised to see a missionary come out of the forest from that direction. They marveled that the Gringses had entered their territory by that seldom-traveled route.

One of the officials spoke English perfectly and Herbert explained to him that he wanted to open a mission station in a part of the tribe where the people were entirely out of touch with civilization. From this man Herbert learned that the Bankutu tribe had an estimated population of 32,000 people. The official said that two or three of the villages were very wild and had not yet submitted to the Government. Officials considered the area very dangerous territory.

The officials were dubious about Herbert's desire to enter the area. They warned Herbert, "It will be too dangerous for you to take your family there." Moreover, they warned that it would be very difficult to bring European food in and that the Gringses would have to live almost entirely on the native food.

Herbert assured them that they had already served eight years among the savage tribes of Northeastern Congo and were fully aware of the danger and difficulty. He told them his family could live on the native food and that God had recently brought them through a shipwreck in the ocean and other hardships. He told them that the God who had already done so much for them would enable them to establish a mission station in the Bolongo clan of the Bankutu. The officials relented and the Territorial Administrator sent police to call porters and bring the family to a large village near the government post Oshwe, where they remained for a few days.

About the middle of January 1934, the family started for the Bolongo clan of the Bankutu tribe, a trip of ten days' portage from Oshwe to Lokolama. They passed through many big villages where the people had never before seen a white woman and children. Sometimes the native women called Bessie and Louise "bekaji" (spirits or ghosts) and pulled their long hair or pinched them to see if they were really flesh and blood. The girls sweetly endured such treatment and quickly learned enough of the language to talk to the women and girls and tell them about Jesus. The official left one of his black soldiers with them in the village, not so much to protect them as to keep the people from running away for fear of the "bekaji."

The Grings family stayed in the village of Lokolama while Herbert began looking for a station site. He rode his bicycle further east through forest and plain, passing through four villages until he came to the village Mbongo. There he met an intelligent headman named Kankai. The Belgian government had taken Kankai out of his village as a young man and trained him to be a soldier in World War I. Kankai spoke three languages–Kingwana, Lingala and his own language, Lonkutu. Here was a man who could not only interpret for Herbert but who was also acquainted with the outside world and the white man's ways. From Kankai they learned of two more villages to the east and a path leading north from Mbongo to Munja, the village of big chief Zulu-mpembe. Plainly this was the center of the Bolongo clan. This was where God wanted them!

Herbert went back and brought Ruth and the children to Mbongo where spears and drawn bows and arrows greeted them. The tribesmen surrounded them. Louise, age five at the time, tried to hide behind her mother's skirt, though she found it not much protection. The spokesman for the tribe wanted to know why they were there. God gave Herbert wisdom to handle the situation well as he explained why they had come. At first the people did not want the Grings family there. Up to this time, all they knew of white men was what they had observed when the Belgian government agent would come with soldiers and guns for the yearly tax collection. Not only did they have to give him taxes, but they also had to serve him without pay while he was in their village.

The Grings family settled among the tribe and had no further trouble with them as the people quickly saw the difference in the way the missionary family behaved compared to the government official. They made their home in a little government guesthouse while Herbert built their first temporary house of poles, thatch and bark. They decided to build the house in a large grove of trees in the middle of a small plain. This would be an ideal place to escape the heat of the tropical sun. Herbert hired village men to make a clearing in the midst of the trees, just big enough for their house. The men brought building materials from the forest and Herbert began to build their house.

All was not smooth going, though. Herbert became ill with some kind of stomach trouble and could eat nothing except a little gruel or soup. The native people had brought them many bananas and ripe plantains. The rest of the family ate them freely while Herbert could not eat even one. He continued working on the house as much as he could without food until his legs wasted away to "pipe stems," and he had to lie on his bed. The natives thought he would die, but Herbert said, "I'm not going to die. I'm going ahead and build the mission station!"

The next morning a man from a distant village appeared at the door with a large bunch of spinach greens to sell. He had heard of a new white family at the Mbongo village and had traveled two days to bring the spinach greens to sell to them. After a few meals of the tender spinach, Herbert's stomach trouble cleared up and he could eat again as usual. God had once more been watching over his faithful servant! Herbert finished the house in March of 1934.

Besides bananas and plantains, pineapples were abundant. Wild antelope and pig meat, which they could buy from the natives very cheaply, were also plentiful. The Gringses learned to like the native "Kwanga" bread, made from the fermented and steam-cooked roots of the cassava plant. Some of the villages in the adjoining Bolendo clan had rice they could buy. In place of sugar, they bought large gourds full of wild honey. The one thing that was hard to get was salt, so they were thankful they had brought in a large supply of rock salt when they came and used it to trade for eggs and chickens.

CHAPTER 12

A NEW WORK AND A GREAT LOSS

With the food and house problem solved, Herbert began leaving Ruth to run the station and school they had started while he went on preaching trips to the villages for a week or more at a time. One or more of the children always accompanied him. The Grings children were a vital part of the ministry. They were a great attraction to the African people, and they loved sharing the Gospel with them. They helped by telling Bible stories to the native children. Many children believed on Jesus as their Savior as a result.

Two young lads, Bosangi and Bashomia, came from Lomasa village to the east. They wanted to learn to read. They did not come at regular times, yet whenever they came, Ruth would stop whatever she was doing and go outside to teach them, even if she had to leave the meal table. They were quick learners and soon started going with Herbert on preaching trips.

As others became interested and learned to read, Herbert found it necessary to make a translation of the Gospel of Mark so they could have at least part of God's Word in their own language. Herbert and Ruth prayed for a language helper.

One morning a fine looking man, Bosesa-nkoi, dressed in short pants and light colored shirt and wearing a tropical sun helmet, came to their door. He said he wanted to work for them. He told them he was dragged into the Belgian Army and was sent as a soldier in World War I to British East Africa. Bosesa-nkoi spoke three languages and he had attended meetings of other missionaries. He could read and write. He worked as secretary to Chief Zulu-mpembe, and now he wanted to work for a man who "had a heart like his heart." He became Herbert's faithful helper and together they translated the Gospel of Mark, songs and Scripture verses into the Lonkutu language. He eventually went back to his distant village to share Christ and died there. A man named Bosangi took his place and helped Herbert translate the Book of Acts.

In the years at the Mbongo station, only one white person besides the government official ever visited the Gringses. Ruth did not see another white woman for nearly two years, until she made a four-week trip with her son, Roy, to Oshwe to share Christ with the people there. From Oshwe they went further to the Swedish Baptist Mission in the Basakata tribe where another white woman missionary lived. What a blessing Ruth had, spending time with another woman of a similar background!

Soon after she got back home, Ruth became ill with the black-water fever, a complicated form of malaria carried by mosquitoes. The nearest doctor was at Oshwe. It would require twenty days for a messenger to go, get the doctor and get back. Herbert realized how useless it would be to send for him.

Herbert and the children sat by Ruth's bed, cared for her, and watched and prayed. For a time Ruth seemed to be recovering. She even got out of bed when an emergency call came from a nearby village for her to help a woman in childbirth. She went and helped deliver the baby, but when she returned home, she went back to bed and soon lost consciousness. She could not even swallow a spoonful of water. "Like a candle burning lower and lower, her life burnt out," wrote Herbert. In the early afternoon, June 21, 1936, while Bessie and Louise sat by their mother's bedside and Herbert took a short rest, Ruth moved for the last time. She moved into her eternal home with her Savior whom she had served so faithfully on earth.

The family was heartbroken. They sat together around the table of their small mud-brick house and tried to comfort one another with God's Word. What sorrow filled their hearts! Herbert could not imagine how he could carry on without Ruth. She had been his faithful and loving wife, and his devoted co-worker and confidant. He knew he had to trust God for strength or he could not go on bearing the complete burden of his family and the ministry alone. The children needed him. What would they do without their mother? And God's work must go on. Many African people still needed to hear the Gospel.

That afternoon Herbert and the boys chose a grassy place at the edge of their grove of trees, and Robert and Roy dug a grave. The next morning two of the village men carried Ruth's body on a cot to the little chapel Herbert had built near the village. All the people gathered for the funeral service. They stood stunned and silent! The white Bible Woman had not been able to escape death's fearful grip any more than they could. They had never seen such a funeral before, and they were amazed at what they saw. Though the Grings family wept tears of grief, they made no loud shouting and wailing like the natives did over their dead. They did not throw themselves on the ground, twisting and screaming pleas that their own lives might be spared. The family sang hymns, prayed and talked to the people about the happy home in Glory where "Mama's" spirit had gone. Herbert promised them that they, too, could go to that beautiful village of God if they put their trust in the blood of Jesus Christ to save them. The funeral service was a testimony to the natives and was used of God to change some of their lives.

The people asked to look upon the dead body. Herbert uncovered Ruth's face and the native men, women and children passed by her body. They looked with wonder and respect upon the cold, calm, white face of the one who had often told them about Jesus and taught many of them to read. Two of the men carried the body to the grave where they placed it in a hollowed-out log that had served to catch rainwater, and covered it with a slab of wood for a lid. With more hymns and prayer, they buried Ruth in that far away jungle grave and in the following years, her grave was a silent testimony for Jesus Christ.

The people went back to their huts without a word. It seemed they still did not understand. However, after a few days, the five young men who had come most often to have "Mama" teach them to read, often at inconvenient times and with no regularity, showed up at the mission house. They told Herbert they wanted to believe. When Herbert questioned them about their decision, they said, "Now we know that believing in Christ is good for dying. What you preached these years sounded good for living, but we didn't know it would help at death's advent." They had witnessed the reality of Christ's power over death. They believed, followed the Lord in baptism, and went forth to share the great things God had done for them.

Ruth left a special monument behind for the people she had loved. She had planted two beautiful palm trees at the village of Mimia and had brought the seed back with her from a preaching trip down by the Lokoro River. The trees grew and flourished. The people would point to them and say, "Those are Mama's palms. She told us about Jesus."

CHAPTER 13
CLOSE CALLS

Herbert had to go to Oshwe with witnesses to report Ruth's death to the Territorial Administrator. He left Bob, Roy and Mark with Bosesa-nkoi to teach the school and to keep the mud-brick house he had built for Ruth just two months before her death. He took Bessie and Louise with him for the twenty-one day trip to and from Oshwe. Bessie had learned to ride her own bike and Herbert carried Louise on his bicycle. In each village they entered, the girls were the main attraction. Herbert preached to large crowds of people in each village.

Both humans and wild animals were always dangers along the trails. Herbert and the children would frequently see the wild animals. The animals usually left them alone, however, unless they felt threatened. Occasionally, Herbert or the children would have a close call.

PYGMIES

Sometimes the family would stop to preach in Pygmy villages. The people there were not always friendly to outsiders. In one large Pygmy village, the little people became very agitated and began to murmur among themselves. A headman shouted in Herbert's ear, "Run or they will kill you."

Thankfully, the path out of the village was clear and smooth. Herbert and the girls jumped on their bicycles and soon left the threatening mob behind. A year or so later Roy and Herbert also had a narrow escape from one of the Pygmy villages. Most of the tribes were friendly, though, and numbers of the people accepted Christ as their Savior.

Bob and Roy volunteered to take their bicycles and cooking pot, and go out to preach the Gospel in other distant villages. About that time, five more of the young men whom Ruth had taught to read asked Herbert to baptize them, and he also trained them to open regular schools in their villages. Herbert visited the schools occasionally to help, limiting his time to day trips because he could not leave the younger children alone. For this reason, the family decided to close the station, take only what belongings were necessary, and just travel from village to village, preaching and teaching. For many months, they traveled with the whole family participating in the ministry. Herbert and the older boys would preach; the little girls told Bible stories.

As Bessie grew and became more expert at riding her bicycle, she carried Louise on a seat in front of her. At one village, Herbert bought the children a little black chick for a pet. The girls carried it in a little basket on their bicycle. When they would arrive at a rest house, they would put the little chick down and hunt roaches and termites to feed it. It followed them everywhere they went. They named it "Little Black Peep."

One day, Bessie told the story of the rich man and Lazarus to the natives in a village where they were staying. She said that Lazarus had died and the angels carried him into Abraham's bosom where he was happy and content. Just then, Black Peep, who had been scratching in the dust in front of her, turned over on his back with his feet in the air and twittered in contentment. The natives watched with interest. Then Bessie told how the rich man died and in hell he lifted up his eyes and said, "Father Abraham, send Lazarus to dip his finger in water and cool my tongue for I am in torment in this flame." Bessie wailed the rich man's words in such a terrifying way that Little Black Peep jumped up, ran and hid behind her. The natives all laughed, for Black Peep had helped to illustrate that hell is a fearful place.

In 1937, after successfully preaching the Gospel in three villages surrounding the government post at Bena-Bendi on the Kasai River, the family decided to establish a mission station among the Boldi clan at Topoka-Tope. At Basongo, which was across the river and about twenty miles away over a rough, hilly road, was another large government post with shops and mail communications. They could go on their bicycles one day, get mail and provisions and return home the next day. Port Francqui, at the center of the Cape-to-Cairo Railroad, was also only two days away. Hundreds of people in this territory had never heard the Gospel. God blessed this move and many people heard of the love of God for the first time.

Fire

One day Herbert took Louise with him on his bicycle and went to Basongo to get their mail. The next day about noon they passed through a big plain on their way home. This was during the dry season when new, tender grass shoots appeared and the animals came to graze. Yearly, hunters set fire at the edge of the plain to drive the antelope out where they could shoot them with their bows and arrows. A fire had been set that day but it was burning lazily and there was no wind. Herbert sensed no danger and rode on into the midst of the plain with Louise behind.

Suddenly a wind sprang up and the flames came leaping towards them. The smoke became dense, obscuring their view.

Herbert tried to pedal faster to get ahead of the fire, but his chain jammed. He jumped off and pushed the bicycle. The fire was rapidly coming nearer. Herbert left the path and tried to push the bicycle through the long grass. The fire leaped over the narrow path and raced toward them. The smoke was so dense that Herbert could not see which way to go.

Just then a voice whispered in his ear, "This way! This way!" Herbert recalled the words of Isaiah 30:21, "This is the way, walk ye in it." He followed the Holy Spirit's guidance and immediately came to a tall patch of green grass. He and Louise ran into it, standing quietly as the fire swept by on both sides of them. When it was past and the smoke cleared away, they looked all around them over the blackened plain. No other spot of green grass was in sight. Although their throats were parched, they were unharmed. Not even a spark had fallen on Louise's dress. Then they remembered Isaiah 43:2, "When thou walkest through the fire thou shalt not be burned, neither shall the flame kindle upon thee."

The Python

One day Herbert was opening a path through the ravine to their water spring at the Topoka-Tope station. Two native men were following him to clear the path with their bush knives. As they neared the spring in the dense jungle, Herbert heard "swish-swish." He went a little further and heard the sound again. He stepped up onto a little elevation where he could see down into the spring, and there a great python lay coiled. She had swallowed an antelope and her middle was so swollen and heavy that she could not crawl away. She raised her head and three or four feet of her body up above her swollen belly, ready to strike out in defense.

Herbert called the men to come with their bush knives but they were afraid to approach the great python. Impatient at their delay, Herbert took one of their bush knives, cut a long pole and sharpened the end. Then he approached the python. She struck out with her mouth wide open to grab him and draw him into her coils. He jabbed the pole into her mouth and held her to the ground until one of the men came and hacked off her head.

The python was over twelve feet long and so heavy that they had to tie her to a pole and carry her up to the plain. They opened her belly and pulled out the dead antelope, which had horns six inches long and weighed about forty pounds. The python also had twenty or more eggs in her belly.

Herbert used the illustration of the python to preach a sermon to the people. "You see," he said, "she came to her death because she swallowed up the antelope and could not crawl away. That is the way it is with Satan. He swallowed up the Lord Jesus on the cross and now Satan cannot escape. He is a defeated enemy. This antelope is dead and we took it out of the snake's belly, yet we know the Lord Jesus is alive. He arose from the dead and now death has no more power over a believer."

ENCOUNTER WITH AN ELEPHANT

On one trip through the forest, Herbert, Bob and Roy had ridden for two days on their bicycles. At night they slept in the forest with a fire burning on each side of them to ward off the wild animals. During the second night, they heard elephants, but the elephants smelled their fire and passed by the camp. The next morning Herbert and the boys started out with no further thought of the elephants.

Herbert rode into a ravine ahead of the boys. Suddenly he heard a great scream like a steamship whistle. He clamped on his brakes and stopped. There at the side of the road, just a few feet away in the underbrush was a mother elephant with her baby by her side. She looked at Herbert and he at her. He wanted to turn and run back the way he had come, which probably would have caused her to chase him and trample him to death. Instead, the verse in Genesis 9:2 came to his mind, "The fear of you and the dread of you shall be upon every beast of the earth." Instead of running, Herbert said in his heart, "Lady elephant, I know you are afraid of me. If you won't do me any harm, I won't do you any harm." Then he slowly walked and pushed his bicycle by her. She let him pass. Herbert then motioned for the boys to follow. The mother elephant let them pass. Then the baby elephant ran off into the forest and the mother followed it. The great beast could have easily killed them all but the Lord held her back.

CHAPTER 14
ALONE AGAIN

Missionary friends advised Herbert to put the girls and Mark in a school or a place where they would have white women to care for them. Herbert loved his children dearly and the idea of separating from them did not appeal to him at all. As he prayed and thought about it, he decided it was best to follow his friends' advice. After making this heart-wrenching decision, finally Herbert placed the three younger children with other missionaries who would care for them and teach them along with their own children. Bob and Roy stayed with their father, helping with the ministry.

They had already moved back to work with the people in the Bolongo and Bolendo villages. During the next year, Herbert baptized over five-hundred converts and organized them into local churches with leaders who could read and teach them God's Word. He also established schools. Two different missionary groups printed copies of Herbert's translations of the Gospels of Mark and John, so many of the believers who had learned to read had the printed Scriptures and typewritten copies of hymns in their own languages. The natives knew Herbert affectionately as "Tata Mandefu" (Father Beard).

One old man whom Herbert baptized came to trust the Lord Jesus because of the testimony of his slave. In years past, the two men's tribes had been at war with each other. The old man, a strong warrior at the time, captured a boy and made him his slave. As a young man, the slave converted to Christianity at one of Herbert's meetings. His life changed so much that the old man came to know the Lord, also.

He said to his slave, "You used to be lazy and disobedient. You would steal and lie to me and do many bad things. Now you work and do what I tell you to do. You don't steal and tell me lies. How is it?"

The young man told him it was because he had given his heart to the Lord Jesus who had washed it and made it clean through His blood. "Now I want to please my Savior by pleasing you."

After a while, Bob went away to Bible school at Glenvar, Cape Town, South Africa. Thus, Herbert lost his main helper and companion for the work in the Congo. Only Roy was now with his father. However, he, too, soon went out on his own. On a trip to South Africa, Herbert and Roy stopped to see Bessie, Louise and Mark at the mission school they now attended at Lubondai. Roy decided to stay and attend the school while Herbert went on to South Africa alone, expecting Roy to rejoin him on the return trip. Instead, when Herbert got back to the Congo, he learned that the American Consul at Leopoldville had drafted Roy for service in World War II. Herbert was now all alone—again.

Herbert took his bicycle and started out to revisit all of the Bankutu villages. What a lonesome and heart-breaking trip Herbert had, coming to the familiar places where he and his family used to sit down in the forest to eat their food, or the little streams where they bathed, or where they stopped to pray before entering a village to preach to the people! Sometimes there was such a lump in his throat that he couldn't even drink water.

At Christmas time Herbert went to see Bessie, Louise and Mark. They prayed for God's will regarding the possibility of a return trip to the United States. They prayed that God would send them three-thousand dollars to pay passage for the four of them. When Herbert returned to his mission station, he received a letter from his lawyer saying that his mother had deposited three thousand dollars in a bank several years earlier before she died. The money was still there, and it belonged to Herbert! Because of the war, the bank could not send the money out of the country, but Herbert could use it to buy passage on a steamship. God had shown it was his will for them to return to the United States for a while.

Herbert returned to the Topoka-Tope station with a lighter heart. He wrote to Bob who was returning to the Congo to work under another mission organization, asking him to get permission to come for a month or so and make a final visit with Herbert to the Bankutu villages. He also wrote to Bessie and asked her to cut her schoolwork short and come with Bob when he passed through on the train. They decided that Louise and Mark would stay and finish their schoolwork.

CHAPTER 15
BITTEN BY AN ADDER

At the time the family had left their house at Topoka-Tope, they couldn't lock it up to prevent stealing, so they dug a cellar in the bedroom and put their trunks and household supplies in it. They laid logs over the top and covered it smoothly with clay so that no one would see a cellar there. When Herbert returned home after his visit with the children, he opened up the cellar to let it air out. The next evening he stepped barefooted down into the loose sand of the cellar and picked up a trunk. As he did, he felt something sting his heel.

He jumped out of the hole and looked at his heel. There were two drops of blood about half an inch apart. He took a light and looked into the cellar, where he saw a small, poisonous adder that had bitten him in the heel. Herbert killed the adder with a bush knife and put it in a tin can on the table so that if he died from the bite people would know what had killed him.

The poison burned like fire in his heel and soon he began vomiting. He felt his heart flutter and thought his end had come. He knelt down and told the Lord that he was not afraid to die because he knew the Lord Jesus had saved him. Then it seemed as if Heaven opened and he could see the Beautiful City. He wanted to go, until a little voice whispered in his heart, "But what will become of your children who expect you to meet them at the railroad station?"

Herbert prayed, "Yes, Lord, for my children's sake, heal me of this snakebite."

He felt a pressure in his right side and he vomited blood. He was sure now, however, that he would not die. He managed to pull the heavy wooden table near the window and lay down on it where anyone passing by the house could see him. He had a long, torturous night, filled with pain and sickness. At times his mind was a whirl of memories, as if his whole life played out before him, though not necessarily in chronological order. He remembered his childhood, when he became a Christian. He remembered his mountain ministry in California, his call to Africa, different events in his life as a missionary. He remembered Ruth and his children. When he could keep his mind in focus, singing hymns and praying helped him resist the devil throughout the long night.

The next morning he resolved to go meet Bob and Bessie in spite of his still swollen heel that burned like fire. He loaded his bicycle with a few supplies and started riding, pedaling with one foot when the path was level, hopping along and pushing the bicycle when it was uphill. It took him two hours to get to the first village. The natives there helped him get to the Kasai River where he found a canoe waiting. He passed over to the motor road on the other side and finally got to Port Francqui where he was to meet his children's train.

The poison had made a red streak up his right side and he had a lump the size of a large bean near the back of his head. He found a doctor who gave him an injection of antivenom, which stopped the poison. He slowly recovered but his foot was numb for a long while. Bob and Bessie came on the train and rejoiced that God had spared their father's life.

CHAPTER 16
RETURN TO AMERICA

Herbert, Bob and Bessie went on bicycle through the Boldi, Bolendo, Bolongo and Isoldu clans, preaching, baptizing hundreds of people, giving the Lord's Supper and bidding farewell to their beloved Bankutu people. When they arrived at Bosanja, Bob bid the rest of the family goodbye and rode away on his bicycle to join his new missionary partner. Several years would pass before Herbert would see his oldest son again.

Herbert and Bessie turned their bicycles and made the long, weary trip to Mangungu where they joined Louise and Mark. A missionary friend took them by car from there to Kikwit where they obtained passage on riverboats to Leopoldville. There they tried to get passage on a ship to the United States. It was, however, at the close of World War II and many people were trying to return to Europe. One had to have priority to get passage on a ship. Herbert asked the immigration officer for a visa so he could go back to the Congo when he was ready to leave America, but the man put him off saying that he could get the visa in Belgium.

The Grings family decided to make their way to Pointe Noire in French Equatorial Africa and try to get passage from there. In Pointe Noire they had to rent rooms and wait for several weeks before passage was available. While they waited, Herbert preached on board ships and in the city prison.

At last they got passage on a big, U.S. army troopship on loan to Belgium. The girls and Mark stayed in a big compartment with two hundred or more women and children. Herbert had to go to a men's compartment with triple deck bunks. He seldom saw his children. Though he had looked forward to spending this time with them after they had been apart so long, he was pleased that they had other missionary children for companions and were happy and content.

When they arrived at Antwerp, Belgium, the family got a room at the Salvation Army headquarters. Herbert sent word of their location to Roy who was stationed in Germany. Roy obtained a leave of absence and came to spend a few days with them. What a glad reunion it was for all of them, and how fine Roy looked in his soldier's uniform.

Again, Herbert could not secure a return visa to the Congo and again passage on a ship was very difficult to get. Then one day while he was out looking for passage, a big U.S. liberty ship tied up near the quay where the Gringses were staying. Bessie and Louise saw the big American flag waving and went out unaccompanied to walk on the quay and look at the ship. Police in plain clothes mistook them for "adventurous" young girls and hauled them off to the police station. Upon learning that they were the daughters of missionaries to the Congo, the police inspector interrogated them separately about what they believed. While the inspector questioned one girl, the other witnessed to the men in the outer office, giving them the Gospel. Many of the policemen listened and the police inspector was convinced of the truth. Bessie ended up by saying to the others, "We'll bring you a Bible and prove it to you." The police released the girls without further incidence. The next day they took Bibles and Testaments to the police station and Herbert preached to the men there.

Herbert told the American captain of the U.S. liberty ship that he had served in the U.S. Navy and he was a missionary in the Congo. Now he was trying to bring his motherless children back to the U.S. for their education.

The captain brought his fist down on the table with a bang and said, "I am the captain of this ship and if anybody goes as passengers, you and your children do!"

Even with the captain's help, though, it was difficult to get around all the regulations. Finally, one day, word came that they could sail. Another missionary family and two of Bessie and Louise's schoolmates sailed on the ship also, and they had happy times together crossing the Atlantic.

After the ship landed at Baltimore, Maryland, God provided transportation and accommodations for the family until they could make their way across the country, and they could place the children with relatives and friends for their care and education. Again, Herbert was very reluctant to say goodbye to his children, yet he knew it was for the best. For a while, he traveled, visiting old friends and giving missionary lectures in churches and private homes, though his heart was still in Africa. Once again, he decided to find passage and embark for the land he loved.

This time it was apparently God's will to close the door. When Herbert arrived at Boma, the entrance port of the Congo, the immigration officer came aboard and took Herbert and his baggage off the ship. Without giving Herbert a reason, the officer told Herbert that he could not enter the Congo. Herbert tried everything he could think of to find a way to reenter the Congo. He contacted government officials and the American Consul, and enlisted missionaries' help. Finally he received a letter from the American Consul saying permission was denied because, "You are an undesirable person." Herbert believed that a large religious group had influenced the government because they did not want Baptist missionaries in the country.

Herbert stayed at Boma, hoping and praying that a way would open for him to return to the Bankutu people. After three months, he received orders to take passage on a steamship back to Antwerp. He stayed there all winter while he appealed his case to the colonial minister. While he waited, God opened up a door to put Gospel literature and Scripture portions on board the many ships that entered the port. He visited an average of three ships a day, five days a week, giving the Gospel to the crews of more than a thousand ships of twenty-one nationalities in about six months. Most men would graciously accept the literature, but American seamen would often throw the tracts out of the porthole or tear them up.

In February of 1948, at the invitation of a missionary friend, Herbert went to Norway. With his friend as an interpreter, he went to homes and churches telling about his missionary work in the Congo. The newspapers printed some of his missionary articles. In August, he went to Holland to attend an International Conference of Christian Churches. When he tried to get church leaders to help him get back into the Congo, he found they could not help at that time. It seemed the only thing left to do was to return to the United States.

Upon arriving in the U.S., Herbert went to the Bureau of African Affairs in the State Department in Washington, D.C. The head official gave Herbert a long, personal interview, saying all he could do was get him a temporary tourist visa to visit the Congo. Herbert sadly gave up all hopes of returning and went to California where all the children except Bob were now attending either Bible College or high school. After a sweet visit with them, he again started out to share his burden for Africa in churches, homes and everywhere people were willing to listen. Many hearts were touched to pray, give and go to the mission field. God would open other doors for Herbert Grings, yet his heart would always be in his beloved Africa.

CHAPTER 17

HOME AGAIN

In the fall of 1948, Herbert boarded a bus going to Santa Maria, California. He sat next to a man from Mexico who had come to California to earn money by picking fruit. Herbert showed him some of his African pictures. The man said, "Down in Mexico we have some Indians like that who live near my orange orchard in the State of Sonora." He went on to say that his house was vacant and that Herbert could live in it if he wanted to visit the Yaqui Indians. Thus began a new ministry in Central and South America.

Through a chain of Christian friends, Herbert became acquainted with a group who did gospel recordings. The group gave him gospel records in the Spanish and Yaqui languages and another Christian friend gave him an old Victrola. He secured a six-month visa for Mexico and started out for his new field of missionary service. He spoke no Spanish or any other language in which he had recordings, but the Victrola spoke the languages perfectly. He played his records in shops and homes, on the streets or anywhere it was convenient to do so. After two months, he had to vacate the house where he was living, so he discovered where the Yaqui Indians were camped, and walked from one shelter to another, playing the records and preaching with what few words he had learned. Many of the Indians gladly received the Gospel message.

Because Herbert's six-month visa was running out, he went into Belize. From there he went to the Grand Cayman Islands, Jamaica and Puerto Rico. Herbert ended up spending sixteen years in Central and South America, preaching the Gospel in every country and visiting some of them two or three times, penetrating into the jungles as much as possible. He would frequently write his children saying he had a guide who would take him far into the interior to Indian headhunters and if they didn't hear from him again, they would know that he had given his life for the Gospel.

His most extensive ministry was in Brazil. Although he learned to speak some Spanish and Portuguese and was able to translate key verses into some of the Indian languages, the Gospel recordings were his greatest means of communication. Hundreds of people put their faith in God's Son, Jesus Christ. Still Herbert longed to be back in Africa.

During these sixteen years, the children all grew up, married and returned to the Congo as missionaries. After eleven years, Louise and her husband, Darrell Champlin and their family left Africa and reopened an abandoned mission field in Surinam, South America. Herbert visited them there in 1967. Seeing how much he still longed to be in Africa, they suggested he try at least to visit his other children and their families there. Encouraged, Herbert immediately set about making his plans. God opened doors and in November of 1967, he stood once more on African soil.

Whether or not the government would allow him to remain was another question. Many years of political upheaval had taken place on the continent. The Congo was now Zaire. The country was experiencing a new freedom but had no idea how to handle it. Herbert's staying depended much on the immigration officer who interviewed him and how much of a bribe the man would require. Herbert had nothing to offer the man, so he did what he had always done. He prayed and trusted the matter to God.

When Herbert met with the officer, the man held a form he was required to fill out. The officer asked what Herbert planned to do in Zaire. Herbert told him he was a missionary. He asked what mission board sponsored him. Herbert replied, "None."

Next, the man asked where his station was.

Herbert said, "I do not have one."

The officer asked where he would get the money to live.

Herbert replied, "God gives me my money."

The officer was flustered. He could not fill in the blanks with appropriate answers. He looked at Herbert and said, "What does an old man like you want to do in Zaire?"

Herbert told him, "My wife is buried here. I want to die in Africa and be buried with her."

The officer gave Herbert full permission to enter the country and to go anywhere he wished for as long as he wished to stay! God had indeed opened the door and Herbert was home at last!

After visiting with his family, Herbert returned to the area where he and Ruth had ministered after they returned from their first trip back to the U.S. He again walked or biked the trails into the distant villages, preaching the Gospel and ministering to "his" beloved people. Although some of the believers he had led to the Lord years before had gone to be with the Lord, their children and grandchildren as well as other believers he had previously introduced to Jesus greeted him. "Father Beard" had returned. They happily welcomed him back. The amazing thing was that after all those years he could still speak the languages he had learned when he first came to the Congo and could easily communicate with the people.

Herbert was an old man now, though, and Louise was concerned that he would die alone along one of the trails with no one knowing for perhaps days or longer. Perhaps the wild animals would carry off his body and they would never recover it. She prayed, "Lord, please do not allow my father to die alone on some lonely forest trail. Please allow one of his children to be with him when he dies."

Herbert served the Lord in Zaire (Congo) for ten more years. Then in 1977, he traveled to the south to visit Roy in the capital city, Kinshasa. While there he became ill with pneumonia and was hospitalized. Bob was also visiting in Kinshasa, so both of his oldest sons were with Herbert in his last hours. Another special person was there, too. Pambo, the son of one of the first five believers whom Herbert and Ruth brought to the Lord at Mbongo, was with him. Herbert's sons and Pambo read the Scriptures, prayed and sang to him. On November 7, 1977 at the age of eighty-five, Herbert left his body and joined Ruth in Heaven to give honor to the Savior whom he served for so many years, in many places, in many ways and in spite of many obstacles. His attitude had always been, "Never turn back; keep preaching God's Word." He had served his Savior faithfully, sacrificially and humbly, and had loved the souls of men fervently.

Herbert could not be buried with Ruth, who was buried a thousand miles interior at Mbongo. Travel was still very rugged and too difficult and long to take Herbert's body there for burial, but what did it matter? Herbert and Ruth were reunited again in Glory. They were both "at home," both in the Congo and in Heaven.

EPILOGUE

This book would not be complete without mention of the ongoing ministry of Herbert Grings to this day. Not only are there many believers, churches and schools on the continents of Africa and South America who owe their beginning and continuation in the Christian faith to Herbert and Ruth, but there are also countless servants of God who are reaching others with the Gospel of Jesus Christ and supporting missions because of their influence. Their extended family now numbers eighty-three descendants. Over sixty of these are on the mission field, into the fifth generation.

All of their children, except Grant, and all except four of their grandchildren became missionaries. Grant went to be with the Lord in 1930 as a child while they were in the United States, and Roy entered Heaven on January 4, 2006 from the Congo. Mark joined his parents and two brothers in Heaven on June 13, 2008 while serving in the country of South Africa.

God greatly used his servants, Herbert and Ruth Grings, and they would be the first to want to give God the glory for all they accomplished. Herbert began his autobiography with these words from one of his favorite hymns:

"Only a sinner saved by grace,
Only a sinner saved by grace,
This is my story,
To God be the glory,
I'm only a sinner, saved by grace."

And truly, that is the secret of a successful Christian life… being a humble servant of God, willing to serve Him wherever and however He chooses, and remaining faithful unto death. For this kind of Christian, there is "No Turning Back."

CPSIA information can be obtained at www.ICGtesting.com
Printed in the USA
BVOW010552160312

285273BV00001B/24/P